Don Quixote

D1421627

Original story by Miguel de Cervantes
Retold by Sally Prue
Series Advisor Professor Kimberley Reynolds
Illustrated by Andy Elkerton

OXFORD
UNIVERSITY PRESS

Letter from the Author

Why did Cervantes decide to write the story of an adventurous knight? Well, perhaps because he was at heart an adventurer himself. He had served as a soldier (surviving being shot three times), had been captured by pirates and had spent five years as a slave.

In spite of all this, most of *Don Quixote*[1] seems to have been written by accident. Cervantes was in prison (not for the first time) for losing some of the King's money in a bank that collapsed, and Cervantes's original idea seems to have been to write a shortish story making fun of tales of knights errant[2]. Fortunately for us, Cervantes grew so interested in his hero that the story ended up rather longer, and it turned out to be about many different things.

Don Quixote was published in 1605 and was a huge success. Not even the fact that most of the first edition was lost in a shipwreck curbed its popularity. *Don Quixote* was a thrillingly new type of book, one that revealed the thoughts of its characters, as well as their actions. This is why *Don Quixote* is often honoured as the world's first novel.

In 1615 Cervantes produced a second volume about the great knight errant and his faithful squire Sancho Panza. Stories from both books are included here.

I hope very much you enjoy them.

Sally Prue

VOLUME ONE

Dear Reader,

I wrote Don Quixote *in prison, which isn't the best place for making beautiful and clever things. This is why it doesn't have any learned footnotes, serious sermons, or start with a poem written by a duke.*

What the book does *have is the story of the brave knight errant Don Quixote and his squire Sancho Panza, who are much more fun than all those serious clever books with sermons in them. I've put in some characters from old stories, too, to show how educated I am.*

Because I couldn't get hold of a duke, I've asked some of the local shopkeepers to rustle up some verses to start things off.

Now, reader, I wish you good health.

Remember me.
Farewell.

Miguel de Cervantes

[1] 'Don Quixote' is pronounced in at least three different ways by English speakers. Usually it's either **Don** kee-**O**-tay or **Don** kee-**HO**-tay. Sometimes, though, people say **Don QUICK**soat.

[2] In ancient legends, a knight errant was a travelling adventurer.

Of all the knights in all the stories,
Don Quixote has most glories.

The squires of old were strong and brave
But Sancho Panza is our fave.

Of horses great and horses fast,
Rocinante's best, if last.

Of ladies praised in song and ditty,
Dulcinea's finest and most pretty.

Chapter One

Don Quixote lived in La Mancha, in a village whose name I can't quite remember.

Well, I'm calling him Don Quixote, but strictly speaking he wasn't actually a don (which is Spanish for 'lord') and his name wasn't actually Quixote, either. But apart from those two small facts, everything written here is completely true and not made up at all; because, as you will see, it's the made-up stuff that causes all the trouble.

Don Quixote lived quite contentedly until one day, he picked up a book about a knight errant. Well, he loved it so much that the moment he'd finished it he started reading another, and after that he couldn't stop. He read silly stories about knights errant day in and day out, until of course in the end his brain shrivelled up and he went mad.

He went so very mad, in fact, that he decided to set out, like one of his storybook knights, to rid Spain of all giants, evil enchanters and other villains. He went and found a suit of armour that had been lying around for centuries, replaced the helmet's missing visor with one he made out of cardboard, and went to find his horse.

The horse was a skinny old thing, but to poor Don Quixote it seemed the finest mount in Spain. He spent four days trying to think of an impressive name for the beast, and ended up with Rocinante. He then spent eight days trying to think of a name for himself: and that's where Don Quixote came from.

It only remained for him to find a beautiful lady to inspire his brave deeds, and to whom he could send any defeated giants.

Unfortunately Don Quixote didn't really know any ladies, but there was quite a good-looking farm girl in the next village, so he decided she'd do. He didn't get round to letting her know she was his lady-love, or to warning her about the incoming giants, but he did make up the name *Dulcinea* for her, which he thought extremely lovely.

That settled, Don Quixote rode out one morning, his shield on one arm and his lance in the other, to put right all the wrongs of Spain.

He hadn't gone far when it occurred to him that only people who'd been officially knighted were allowed to go round killing villains, and for a few dreadful minutes he thought he'd have to go home again. He soon decided, however, that he was bound to come across someone who could make him a knight and so he rode on, his head echoing with all the songs that would one day be written about his adventures.

The July sun soon got so hot that if Don Quixote had had any brains, they'd have melted, and by the time he came to a castle, he and Rocinante were tired out.

At least, Don Quixote *thought* it was a castle: anyone else would have called it an inn.

An inn is used to welcoming strangers, but Don

Quixote, with the cardboard visor and his insistence on talking about giants and knights errant, was stranger than most. Still, everyone was kind. Some ladies helped Don Quixote off with his armour (though not his helmet, because that was held on with green ribbons which Don Quixote wouldn't allow to be cut). The ladies even found him some dripping, which they rubbed into the rustier bits of his armour to help to preserve it. Despite this problem, Don Quixote was only really worried about the fact that he hadn't been officially knighted. He went to the 'lord-of-the-castle' (who was really the innkeeper) and beseeched the man to make him a knight so he could start some serious fighting of villains.

Well, by that time the innkeeper had discovered that Don Quixote had come out without any money, so quite frankly he would have agreed to anything just to get rid of him.

'Knights should always carry money,' he said, crossly. 'Money, food and a first-aid kit for wounds – and they should have a squire to look after them, as well.'

Don Quixote listened humbly as he prepared to stand guard in the courtyard all night, which is what people have to do before they are knighted.

Everyone else settled down to sleep, and everything would have been fine if a mule driver hadn't arrived and needed to use the water trough where Don Quixote had left his armour. Well, the man naturally chucked the heap of old armour onto the ground, and unfortunately his disrespect enraged Don Quixote so much that he gave the poor man a whack over the head with his lance.

The resulting din brought half the people in the inn running, and when they saw the state of the poor mule driver's head they began pelting Don Quixote with stones.

By then, the innkeeper had had more than enough. He tapped Don Quixote on the shoulders with a sword, told him firmly that he was knighted, and opened the door of the inn.

Don Quixote rode out triumphantly, in search of adventure.

Don Quixote was the happiest man alive as he rode along on Rocinante, even though the orders of the 'lord-of-the-castle' meant that he was going to have to head back home to pick up some money, provisions, a first-aid kit and a squire.

Rocinante was happy too, because he was travelling towards his stable, so he went along at quite a good pace, for him.

It wasn't long before they heard howls of anguish and they saw a man hitting a boy. Don Quixote was very angry.

'Discourteous knight!' he exclaimed. 'It ill becomes you to assault an unarmed man. Pick up your lance and fight!'

'Knight?' said the man. 'Pick up my what? Look, this stupid boy keeps losing my sheep!'

'No I don't,' said the boy, quickly. 'He's just trying to make me run away so he doesn't have to pay me. He owes me nine months' pay at seven reals[3] a month already!'

Don Quixote looked very fierce.

'Then you owe this boy ... er ... nine times seven ... er ... seventy-three reals,' he proclaimed. 'Hand them over or die!'

The man couldn't believe this was happening.

'Suppose I take the boy home and pay him there?' he suggested.

'He won't!' said the boy, quickly. 'Don't believe him!'

But Don Quixote sat up even straighter.

'He will not dare to disobey Don Quixote,' he said. 'Have no fear, my boy, this villain will pay you sure enough.'

Then Don Quixote rode away, very happy to have righted his first wrong, and he was in such a daydream about his own bravery, and about his lady-love Dulcinea, that he didn't even notice that that the minute he was out of hearing, the man seized the boy and began hitting him again.

[3] Reals (*say* ray-ahl) were the currency in Spain between the fourteenth century and the nineteenth century.

Chapter Two

It wasn't long after this first adventure that Don Quixote saw six knights coming along the road towards him.

Now, the knights were under the impression that they were really merchants, and so they were surprised when Don Quixote lowered his lance and demanded they declare that Dulcinea was the most beautiful lady in Spain.

'But ... we've never heard of her,' one of them said.

'Have you got a portrait on you?' asked another.

'You must accept Don Quixote's word without proof!' said Don Quixote, ferociously, and charged at the poor merchants.

Terrible things might have happened if Rocinante hadn't tripped and made Don Quixote fall off.

Fortunately the weight of his armour stopped him getting up again, but the merchants were very scared and angry. One of them broke Don Quixote's lance across his back, and then they went off leaving Don Quixote on the ground.

Don Quixote would probably still be there if a farmer hadn't come along and found him lying in the road reciting the adventures of the knight Baldwin.

The farmer put Señor Quixano (for that was Don Quixote's real name) on a donkey and took him home, where his niece, his housekeeper, and his friends, the barber and the priest, were all wild with anxiety about him. They treated Don Quixote's bruises, which he claimed he'd got fighting giants, and carried him to bed. Then, as there was nothing much wrong with him, they left him to sleep and went to his library, where Don Quixote kept the books of knight-errantry that had caused all his problems. First of all, the housekeeper suggested sprinkling the books with water to kill any enchanters that might live inside.

'No, no!' said the niece. 'That's not enough. They must be destroyed!' and she threw them all out of the window, except for a few of the barber's and the priest's favourites, which they saved. They considered keeping the poetry books, but the idea of Don Quixote becoming a poet was even worse than his being a knight, so in the end they just saved the excellent *Galatea* by Cervantes.

They burned the books and had the library door bricked up, and when Don Quixote woke up, his niece told him the whole library had been whisked away by an enchanter.

'Humph,' said Don Quixote. 'I know exactly the one who did it, too. He's afraid I'll fight him.'

'If I were you, I'd stop fighting anyone,' said the niece.

Don Quixote actually did stay quietly at home for a whole fortnight. He talked about knights errant a great deal to his friends, which didn't matter, but unfortunately he also talked about knights errant to a local farm labourer called Sancho Panza, and that turned out to matter a great deal.

Sancho was a good man, but there was no getting away from the fact that he was a complete bird-brain. By the time Don Quixote had talked to him about knight-errantry for a few days, Sancho was so entranced by the promise of riches and power that he'd agreed to become Don Quixote's squire.

Don Quixote sold a few oddments to raise some money, and Sancho helped by providing his own donkey. Don Quixote wasn't sure about the donkey, never having heard of donkeys going on adventures, but in the end it was the best they could do.

Don Quixote and Sancho crept away one evening without telling anyone.

'We'll soon be rich and powerful, won't we?' said Sancho, happily.

'The deeds we are going to do, in six days you'll be governor of an isle[4],' said Don Quixote. 'Or even a king, if you're lucky.'

[4] 'Isle' is a fancy word for an island.

'Oh, really?' said Sancho. 'A king? But look, I'm not sure my wife would be all that good at being a queen. Quite honestly, I think even a countess might be pushing it.'

'You may be sure you'll cope with anything Fate sends you, Sancho.'

It wasn't very long before they came across a group of about thirty windmills.

'Look!' exclaimed Don Quixote. 'Quick! We must kill them at once!'

'Kill who?' asked Sancho, bewildered.

'Over there. With the long arms. Giants.'

'But ... those are windmills, Master.'

'My dear Sancho, how ignorant you are,' said Don Quixote, and he charged full-tilt at the nearest windmill.

It was a windy day, and the sails of the windmills were turning fast. Don Quixote, shouting madly, urged Rocinante at full speed towards the nearest windmill and goodness knows what would have happened if the knight's lance hadn't got caught up in one of the rotating sails. Don Quixote and Rocinante were dragged sideways, pulled off balance, and sent flying.

Sancho arrived as fast as his donkey could take him.

'Didn't I *tell* you they were windmills?' said Sancho, wildly, helping them up.

'An enchanter must have transformed them,' said Don Quixote, rather unsteadily. 'Still, I'll sort him out in the end.'

'Are you all right? You've gone all lopsided.'

'A knight never complains, Sancho, not even if his insides are hanging out.'

'Well, I hope *squires* are allowed to complain,' said Sancho. 'Because after that I need some dinner.'

They spent the night under the trees. Don Quixote was too busy thinking about his lady-love Dulcinea to eat or sleep, but that was all right because Sancho ate and slept for both of them.

'I'm sorry you aren't allowed to join in when I'm fighting giants and other knights, Sancho,' said Don Quixote, as they rode along the next day. 'But I'm afraid that's the rule.'

'Oh, don't worry,' said Sancho. 'I'm quite happy to leave it all to you.'

They hadn't gone far before they saw two monks riding along in front of a fine carriage. Don Quixote got very excited.

'Look!' he exclaimed. 'Two enchanters who've captured a princess!' and he spurred Rocinante forward, shouting, 'Foul creatures! Let her go, or die!'

'Um ... let who go?' asked one of the monks; but Don

Quixote lowered his lance and charged, and if the monk hadn't thrown himself out of the way he might have been seriously injured.

The other monk didn't hang around. He dug his heels into his mule's sides and rode off as fast as he could.

Sancho rode up to the fallen monk and started helping him off with his cloak, and while he was busy a group of travellers arrived along the road and asked Sancho what was going on.

'Oh, my master attacked this monk, so now I'm looting his stuff,' explained Sancho, happily; whereupon the newcomers pushed Sancho roughly out of the way, helped the poor monk back onto his mule, and then they all rode off.

Meanwhile, Don Quixote was talking to the lady in the carriage, who was naturally utterly terrified.

'I, Don Quixote de la Mancha, have saved you from those evil enchanters,' he announced grandly. 'But do not fear, all you have to do to thank me is drive back to Toboso, where my lady Dulcinea lives, and tell her about my bravery.'

Well, that was so peculiar that the lady's bodyguard got seriously worried. He drew his sword, and at once a tremendous fight began. Huge blows were traded back and forth, until at last Don Quixote decided to end the fight once and for all. He raised his sword above his head and rode in for one final mighty blow: but just as he did, the bodyguard raised *his* sword, too, ready for one final mighty blow.

And then—

But unfortunately the records of Don Quixote's adventures finish at that point.

Chapter Three

I found it hard to believe that Don Quixote's superb story should have been abandoned in the middle like that, but that seemed to be the case until one day in Toledo I saw some old notebooks for sale. Now, I'll read anything, even litter, so I picked one up, only to find it was in a foreign language.

Luckily a man beside me looked over my shoulder and began to laugh.

'It says there that the great lady Dulcinea is better at salting meat than any woman in Spain,' he said.

Well, when I heard the name Dulcinea, I had all the notebooks translated, and here they are. They were written by someone called Benengeli, and he seems to have done a good job, except for not praising Don Quixote's wisdom enough.

The main thing to remember is that it's not my fault if there's anything wrong with the rest of the story.

So, back to the fight. Don Quixote's opponent got his blow in first, and it would have been fatal if the blade hadn't twisted in the air and only nearly taken Don Quixote's ear off. Then it was Don Quixote's turn. His sword flashed down, terrifying the bodyguard's mule so much that it reared up and threw its rider.

The bodyguard was now at Don Quixote's mercy, and that might have been the end of him if the lady in the carriage hadn't promised they'd go and find Dulcinea at once.

So Don Quixote rode away quite happily in search of his next incredible adventure.

'Can I be governor of my isle now?' asked Sancho, hopefully.

'Oh, we need to have some more adventures before that,' said Don Quixote. 'For now your job is to bandage my ear. It's a pity I don't happen to be carrying any Balsam of Fierabras on me, for that cures all wounds instantly, even if (as sometimes happens) I've been chopped into several pieces. I only wish it could cure dents in armour, too.'

Sancho and Don Quixote spent that night with some goatherds. As before, Sancho ate and slept well, and Don Quixote ate hardly anything and lay awake all night thinking of Dulcinea.

On the next day, they came across some men digging a grave by the road. It turned out that the man who was to be buried, Grisóstomo, had died for love of a stony-hearted and cruel shepherdess called Marcela.

Grisóstomo's last poem was read out as the grave was dug:

'Although a jewel,
Marcela's cruel,
My cries of pain
Are all in vain.
I'm glad to die,
So no one cry.'

But as Grisóstomo was being laid in his grave a beautiful woman, whom the gravediggers said was the cruel Marcela, appeared on the mountain slope above them.

'Listen, everyone,' she said. 'Do you believe that I should love a man just because he loves me? I've always said that following me about is a waste of time, and I'm saying it again now: if you don't want to be hurt then leave me alone. Then perhaps we can all be happy, and no one need die of hopeless love.'

She left then, and everyone had to admit that she had a point.

Don Quixote thought he'd follow Marcela just in case she needed any knight-errantry doing.

But, as it happened, a new adventure got in the way.

This new adventure was actually Rocinante's fault. Don Quixote and Sancho were having a rest when Rocinante scented some mares and decided to pay them a visit. Well, the last thing the horse-traders who owned the mares wanted was Rocinante coming along disturbing them, so they started to fight him off with sticks.

Don Quixote summed up the situation quickly.

'Those men look like low-born villains, Sancho,' he said. 'That means you can help me fight them.'

'What? But there are twenty of them!'

'I am the equal of a hundred men,' said Don Quixote, sternly.

Unfortunately, though, Don Quixote wasn't the equal of twenty men with sticks, and soon both he and Sancho were so bashed about that the horse-traders got worried and rode off as fast as they could.

'Ouch,' said Sancho, feebly. 'Ow. I wish you had some of that Fairy Brass stuff that cures everything on you, Don Quixote.'

'Remind me never to fight low-born men again,' gasped his master. 'It's not a knight's job. Next time I'll leave it to you.'

'Me? When I've got a wife and children to support? You must be joking. I'm going to forgive everybody everything from now on.'

'You can't forgive everybody if you're a governor, Sancho.'

'Well, at this rate I'm not going to survive long enough to find out. Ouch. Master, is knight-errantry always this bad?'

'Oh no. No, it's usually much worse than this. But

don't worry, dear Sancho, it won't go on long. Remember: death removes all pain.'

When Sancho finally managed to get to his feet, he heaved Don Quixote onto the donkey, and pulled Rocinante upright, too.

Don Quixote was furious when he saw how badly the horse-traders had dented his treasured helmet. He vowed never to eat at a table again until he'd won himself a new one as fine as the helm of Mambrino[5] in the old story. Then Sancho led them on their sorry way to the road to look for somewhere to bathe their wounds.

'Look!' said Don Quixote in delight. 'A castle!'

'It's an inn,' sighed Sancho, but he turned towards it.

The innkeeper wasn't very keen to take in a man who looked as battered as Don Quixote, but Sancho made up a story about falling off a rock, and the innkeeper's wife found Don Quixote a place in the loft.

'He's a knight errant,' Sancho told her. 'And I'm his squire.'

'Well, I wouldn't have known from the look of you.'

'You wait. In a couple of weeks we'll probably both be emperors.'

Don Quixote asked for oil and various herbs and boiled them up together to make some Balsam of Fierabras. Some he put in an old tin, and the stuff that

[5] 'Helm' is an old word for a helmet. Mambrino was a fictional Moorish king who possessed a helmet of pure gold which made its wearer invulnerable.

wouldn't fit in the tin, he and Sancho drank.

The next morning, when they'd both more or less stopped being violently sick, Don Quixote replaced his lance with an iron pike he found leaning against a wall, and said goodbye to the innkeeper.

'Many thanks for the magnificent kindness I have received in your castle,' he said.

'Come off it! This is an inn, not a castle. And *this* is the bill.'

Don Quixote waved it away.

'Knights errant don't pay bills,' he explained. 'The honour of entertaining me is payment enough. Yes, it's quite plain in all the accounts.'

The innkeeper was so surprised he actually did let Don Quixote go, but Sancho wasn't so lucky.

'Me, pay a bill?' Sancho said, as bravely as he could. 'You must be joking. Don't you know *anything* about knight-errantry?'

There's no telling what the innkeeper might have done to Sancho then, but some young men, seeing the chance of some fun, put Sancho on a blanket and started flipping him up in the air on it so roughly that Sancho's screams reached all the way to the road. Don Quixote rode back to the rescue at once, but when he got back to the inn he found he was still too wobbly to get off Rocinante. Unfortunately, shouting commands at the young men had no effect at all.

In the end the young men with the blanket got bored. They put Sancho on his donkey (the innkeeper having taken its saddlebags in payment for their stay) and pushed Sancho, very dizzy, out of the inn.

'I would have saved you, but an enchantment had stuck me to my saddle,' said Don Quixote. 'Would you like some Balsam of Fierabras?'

'What, so I can throw up what guts I've got left?' asked Sancho, bitterly.

'Ah well,' said Don Quixote, 'it's all part of being a knight errant: thrills, spills, winning battles ... '

'I wouldn't know about thrills and battles,' said Sancho, resentfully. 'And as far as I've seen *you* don't either.'

Chapter Four

It was soon after this that Don Quixote noticed two big clouds of dust coming along the road. He went into paroxysms of joy because he was certain they were two armies coming to fight each other over a lady.

They rode up a hill to where they'd get a good view, and Don Quixote gave Sancho a vivid account of the snake-skin armour of one knight, and the silver shield of another.

Sancho peered down and couldn't see any of it.

'But can't you hear the clashing of swords?' asked Don Quixote.

'All I can hear is sheep bleating,' admitted Sancho.

'Sancho, fear has deluded you,' said his master. 'Hey, but look at that! Quick! *Charge!*' and he spurred Rocinante down the hill.

'Stop!' shouted Sancho. 'They're just sheep! *Stop!*'

Well, naturally when Don Quixote started charging the sheep, the shepherds got out their slings and started pelting him with rocks, and hit him so hard that he had to have a swig of the Balsam of Fierabras. The next rock to make contact knocked him right off Rocinante (luckily, it holed the Balsam tin, too) and the shepherds scarpered, afraid they'd killed him.

By the time Sancho reached his master, Don Quixote was throwing up the last of the Balsam.

It was then that Sancho noticed that his saddlebags were missing, and he was so upset he nearly set off straight back home, even though that meant losing both his chances of getting paid and his governorship.

Eventually, Don Quixote recovered enough to get back on Rocinante, and they rode along, sore, tired, and very hungry, because all their food had been in the saddlebags.

It had grown quite dark, and there was still no sign of anywhere to stay, when they saw lights bobbing up and down along the road towards them.

'Ghosts!' whispered Don Quixote, and this time he had some reason for his nonsense because coming along towards them, lit by flickering torches and flanked by riders draped in pale robes, was a cart bearing a coffin.

Don Quixote's hair stood up on end, but he rode forward and hailed the riders.

'Are you mourners?' he demanded. 'Or murderers?'

'We're in a hurry,' said one of the men, shortly, but his rudeness so enraged Don Quixote that he spurred Rocinante forward and knocked the man over, mule and all.

The pale-robed men weren't armed, so all they could do was run like mad, and soon the only one left was the man Don Quixote had knocked over, who'd got trapped under his mule.

'Yield, scoundrel!' said Don Quixote, thrusting forward his pike.

'Yes,' said Sancho. 'Yield to the Knight of the Sad Face!'

'Of course I yield,' said the man, irritably. 'How can I do anything else when I'm stuck under a mule?'

'Then I order you: tell me how this man died!' said Don Quixote, indicating the coffin.

'Of fever.'

Don Quixote took away his pike.

'Of fever, you say? I see. Well ... I suppose as long as it wasn't anything to do with you murdering him then that's all right.'

And once Sancho had slyly stolen some food from the

men's pack-mule, which they'd abandoned in their haste, Sancho helped the man up and said a cheerful goodbye.

Don Quixote and Sancho found a place away from the road and had a feast.

'Look, Sancho,' said Don Quixote. 'Why did you call me the Knight of the Sad Face just now?'

'Well, the teeth those shepherds' rocks knocked out haven't made you any more beautiful,' said Sancho.

'Yes, yes, but do you *have* to talk so much? Can't you be like Sir Galaor's squire Gasabal? *He* was so quiet he's only mentioned once in a whole book.'

'Oh, I'll try,' said Sancho. 'You mistaking those men for murderers will make a good story, though, won't it?'

'No it won't, because people will take it the wrong way,' said Don Quixote, shortly.

Don Quixote led the way back to the road, where who should be coming along towards them but a man with a head that shone like gold. Don Quixote sat up in his saddle.

'He must be wearing Mambrino's helm!' he said. 'You remember, Sancho, the helmet I made the vow about? Here's a chance for glory at last!'

'If I were allowed to speak,' said Sancho, 'I'd point out that knights don't usually ride donkeys.'

But Don Quixote took no notice. He lowered his pike and charged at the poor man, who was a travelling barber wearing his basin on his head to protect his hat from the rain.

All the barber could do was jump off his donkey and run for his life; luckily, he left both the basin and his donkey behind him.

'This is a good basin, too,' said Sancho, picking it up. 'You could get money for this.'

Don Quixote snatched it and put it reverently on his head.

'Good heavens,' he said, 'Mambrino must have had a very big head. And it's a pity the visor's missing.'

'Don Quixote, can I swap my donkey's old saddle for this one?' asked Sancho.

'Well, I've never heard anything in the old stories that says you can't,' said Don Quixote. And so they both rode on quite happily.

'You know what you should do, Master?' said Sancho, after a while. 'You should take service with a king. That'd get you famous in no time.'

'Ah, but a knight must be already famous before a king will take him in,' said Don Quixote. 'Never mind, we'll get to that part of our story, the bit where my royal blood is discovered and you're made a lord, later on ... though I must admit the royal-blood thing isn't going to be easy. Still, the clever man who writes my story may be able to work something out.'

'I'll make a good lord,' said Sancho. 'I've got a lordly figure.'

'Yes, but you'll have to shave,' said Don Quixote.

Later that day they came across a line of chained prisoners destined for the galleys. Don Quixote asked each man why he was imprisoned, and each had a different answer: one for love (of stealing); one for singing like a bird (that is, confessing his crimes); one for playing games (with too many wives).

The last man was wearing even more chains than the others, because he was the notorious villain, Ginés de Pasamonte.

'My dear fellows,' Don Quixote said to the King's guards who were escorting the prisoners. 'These poor men have all been convicted through bad luck or accident. I think you must release them.'

'Release the King's prisoners? That's a laugh,' said a guard – but he stopped laughing when Don Quixote charged him.

Don Quixote fought hard, but the other guards drew their swords and Don Quixote would have been hard-pressed if the convicts hadn't managed to break their chains. Once they were free, all the guards could do was flee for their lives.

'Now we're *really* in trouble,' said Sancho. 'Those were the King's guards you've just beaten up. Quick, run for the hills!'

'First these fine men we've rescued must promise to go to Toboso and tell Dulcinea about my great deed,' said Don Quixote.

Well, then naturally the convicts knocked Don Quixote and Sancho down, took their coats, stamped Don Quixote's basin flat, and ran off leaving Don Quixote and Sancho thoroughly battered, as well as in desperate trouble with the King's guards.

'I should have listened to you, Sancho,' said Don Quixote, at last. 'Low-born men are never grateful. Still, I've learned my lesson.'

'If only,' said Sancho. 'Right, listen to me now, because those guards will be back soon, and if we're not out of here we're dead.'

'If I run away it's only to be kind, because you're afraid,' said Don Quixote. 'I'm not a bit worried myself.'

'We'll go this way,' said Sancho.

They turned off the road and up into the Sierra Morena mountains. It was a wild and lonely place, just right for a knight errant's adventures, and Don Quixote was soon perfectly happy.

Chapter Five

As things turned out, Don Quixote did find an adventure almost at once. Well, it was more of an old rucksack than an actual adventure, but it proved to contain four good shirts, a notebook, and some gold coins.

Don Quixote was only interested in the notebook (it told the story of a man who'd been ditched by his girlfriend for someone richer) so Sancho got the shirts and the money. This perked him up considerably.

A little further on, up on a hill, they spotted a man, long-haired, filthy and tattered.

'He may be the owner of the rucksack,' said Don Quixote. 'You go that way, and I'll go this way, and perhaps we'll catch up with him.'

'Oh no,' said Sancho. 'For one thing I'm too much of a coward, and for another, if it *is* his rucksack I'll have to give the money back.'

So they rode on together and soon they met a goatherd who knew all about the tattered man. He seemed to have been rich, once, because he was always very polite when he begged for food – unless he was having one of his funny turns, when he'd attack people and curse someone called Fernando.

'We must help the poor man,' said Don Quixote, and as luck would have it they came across him almost straight away.

Luckily he was in a polite phase.

'I am Cardenio,' he told them, 'and this is my story. I was just about to get engaged to my lovely Luscinda when the duke summoned me to his castle. His son Fernando had fallen in love with a farmer's daughter, and to separate them the duke wanted Fernando to pay a visit to my home. The trouble was, as soon as Fernando saw Luscinda he was struck with amazement at her good sense and beauty.'

At this point Cardenio had a mad fit, beat up Don Quixote and Sancho, and wandered elegantly away.

Don Quixote got to his feet looking thoughtful.

'Perhaps *I* should go mad with love,' he said. 'Many knights errant do, you know. Roland, for example, killed several shepherds in a fit of sorrow.'

'But Dulcinea hasn't ditched you,' pointed out Sancho, dusting himself off. 'And anyway, poor shepherds!'

'Oh, I wouldn't kill anyone. I'd just hang about weeping until you'd travelled to Dulcinea's house and returned with a letter saying she still loved me. Then I'd go back to being myself again. Hey, you've got Mambrino's helmet safely, haven't you?'

'Well, I've got the barber's basin.'

'Oh Sancho, Sancho, do you *still* not understand enchantment?'

Don Quixote and Sancho slept peacefully that night under a cork oak, but woke to terrible disaster: in the night, the villain Ginés, who was also hiding from the King's guards in the Sierra Morena, had stolen Sancho's donkey. (He didn't steal Rocinante because no one in their right mind would pay money for him.)

Sancho was utterly devastated. He wept, and called the donkey his baby, until in the end, Don Quixote promised that Sancho should have three of Don Quixote's own donkeys when they got home.

Then at last Sancho dried his eyes.

They soon found a meadow where Don Quixote could go mad with love.

'Just wait while I do some mad things, such as tearing my clothes and dashing my head against a rock,' said Don Quixote, 'and then you can head back to Dulcinea's house and tell her about it.'

'Can't you dash your head against something softer?' asked Sancho.

'I'll scribble Dulcinea a letter, and you can get the thing copied out nicely on the way home. It won't matter that it's not in my writing because I don't think Dulcinea can read.'

'You don't know if Dulcinea can read?'

'Well, Corchuelo doesn't like strange men visiting his daughter, so I've only seen her from a distance.'

'Oh, so *that's* Dulcinea! *Corchuelo's* daughter! Ooh, you've chosen a fine strong lass, there ... Hey, what would a farmer's daughter want with all those convicts you tried to send her?'

'Just obey orders, Sancho.'

So Sancho waited while Don Quixote did a couple of demented-looking somersaults, and then Sancho rode away on Rocinante, and Don Quixote started carving hearts on trees and writing verses in the sand of the river bank.

Sancho rode all day, and by nightfall he was glad to spy an inn; unfortunately it was the inn where he'd been blanket-tossed, and he was wondering about finding another place to stay when the priest and the barber from home came out of the inn and recognized him.

Sancho told them everything that had happened, though he couldn't show them Dulcinea's letter because Don Quixote had forgotten to give it to him.

'Never mind,' said Sancho, 'I know it by heart. It starts "Noble and illegal lady".'

'*Regal*, perhaps,' suggested the priest. 'How on earth are we going to get Don Quixote to come home?'

In the end, the priest and the barber decided that the

best way was to dress the priest up as a lady-in-distress, and the barber as her squire. Then the 'lady' would ask Don Quixote to visit her castle, and 'she' would lead him home on the way.

They set out the next morning to pursue their plan, but on the way they realized that they could solve the whole problem without bothering with any dressing-up: all Sancho had to do was tell Don Quixote that Dulcinea wanted to see him.

When they got near the place where Don Quixote was doing his mad-for-love act, Sancho went on alone, leaving the others in hiding. But the barber and the priest had been waiting only a little while when the tattered man Cardenio came along, and as he was having a calm day he told them the rest of his story.

'No sooner had Fernando, the duke's son, set eyes on my lovely Luscinda,' he said, 'than I was called away on business. But while I was away, I heard that Fernando had asked Luscinda's father for her hand in marriage. I rode home speedily and slipped secretly into her house, but only in time to see Luscinda, in her wedding dress, say "I will" before she fainted away.

'Betrayed by everyone, I rushed from the house and never stopped until I reached this wilderness, where I live in misery and madness.'

Cardenio had just finished his sad story when they

heard a voice.

'At last!' it said. 'A wilderness where I can lament my ill fortune!'

And at that moment a shepherd boy came round the corner, took off his hat, and by his long blonde hair revealed himself to be a beautiful woman.

'My dear sir ... or madam,' said the priest. 'Whatever is the matter?'

'Fernando, the duke's son, is the matter,' she answered. 'He said he loved me, and now he has abandoned me.'

At the word 'Fernando', Cardenio broke into a sweat, but luckily he didn't go mad.

'One night, Fernando stole secretly into my house,' the woman told them, 'and he called me by my name, Dorotea.'

Cardenio looked even sweatier when he heard the name Dorotea.

'Fernando told me (and my maid was witness) that his high rank meant that he could declare us married instantly. Because of this, I accepted him as my husband.

'But Fernando's words were false, for not long later news reached me that he had married a woman called Luscinda. Half mad with sorrow, I ran away with a servant to the town where Luscinda lived, only to discover that just before the marriage ceremonies were finished, Luscinda had told everyone that her real love was a man called Cardenio, and then had run away.

'I discovered, too, that my parents, who are rich farmers, were offering a large reward for my return. This aroused my servant's greed, so I pushed him over a precipice and got a job as a goatherd. My master soon saw through my disguise, however, and so, not having another precipice handy, I had to run away. And here you find me, desolate.'

By the time everybody had explained who everyone was to everyone else, Sancho had come back.

'It's no good,' he said. 'Don Quixote says he's not worthy to visit Dulcinea until he's done lots more brave deeds.'

'Well, in that case we'll have to try your original plan for getting him home,' said Dorotea, who was much more cheerful since she'd heard Cardenio's story. 'I can be your lady-in-distress.'

She immediately put on some clothes she'd had with her since she'd left home.

Sancho was amazed at her grandeur.

'Who is *she*?' he asked.

'Er ... she's the Princess Micomicona,' said the priest. 'She's been swindled by a giant and has come to ask for your master's help.'

'Brilliant!' said Sancho. 'If Don Quixote gets in with a princess then we'll *really* be on our way up.'

The barber disguised himself with a beard made from an ox's tail, and then he and Dorotea went off to find Don Quixote.

As soon as Dorotea saw the Knight of the Sad Face, she threw herself at his feet and begged for his help.

'A monster has usurped my kingdom,' she cried tragically.

'Don't worry,' Sancho whispered to Don Quixote. 'It's only a giant. Nothing out of the ordinary.'

Well, Don Quixote was thrilled to bits. He put on his armour at once and they set off. They hadn't gone far (of course the journey to the princess's kingdom was going to take them through Don Quixote's home village) when Don Quixote was spotted by his friend the priest at the side of the road. Cardenio was with him, disguised with a haircut and the priest's cloak.

'My good neighbour!' exclaimed the priest. 'How lucky to meet you!'

'But what are you doing so far from home without your cloak?' Don Quixote asked.

'Um ... well, I was on my way to collect some silver from my cousin in South America, when I was robbed by some convicts that some complete fool had released from their chains,' said the priest (who had heard the story of the convicts from Sancho).

Don Quixote changed colour, but said nothing, and

to fill the silence the 'princess' told them her own story about the Giant Pandafilando, who had forced her to flee her country with just a squire for company. She also mentioned a prophesy that one day she'd marry a brave knight called Don Coyote.

Sancho perked up at this, but Don Quixote shook his head.

'Princess, it cannot be,' he said kindly. 'My heart is all Dulcinea's.'

'Your heart is *what*?' hissed Sancho, unable to believe his ears. 'Oh, come on, Master, you're not going to turn down a *princess*! I mean, she's much better looking than Dulcinea! And how am I going to get my governorship if you don't – *ouch*!' for Don Quixote, enraged, had knocked Sancho down and might have hurt him quite badly if the 'princess' hadn't intervened.

A little way along the road, they came across a peasant with a donkey. Sancho was still looking wistfully at all donkeys, so he recognized this one at once.

He recognized the peasant, too.

'Oi!' he shouted. 'That's my donkey! And that's Ginés the convict, too!'

Well, as soon as Sancho shouted his name, Ginés ran away as fast as he could, and Sancho ran to embrace his donkey with tears of joy.

'Don Quixote and Sancho are terrific, aren't they,' said Cardenio, with great enjoyment. 'No one on earth is clever enough to have made *those* two up!'

Chapter Six

Don Quixote soon had to make friends with Sancho again because he was longing to hear about Sancho's visit to Dulcinea.

'What was Dulcinea doing?' Don Quixote asked, eagerly.

'Um ... sieving wheat in the yard,' said Sancho.

'Ah, but her touch would have turned the grains to pearls. Did she kiss my letter?'

'No ... she just said to shove it on the rack.'

'Wise, lofty lady!'

'Yes, she is quite tall.'

'She wanted to savour it at her leisure, you see. Did you detect a scent of heaven about her?'

'Well, she was quite sweaty. She said she wanted to see you personally.'

'And I must obey Dulcinea, of course, after I've helped Princess Micomicona.'

'But you really won't marry the princess?'

'Don't worry, Sancho, I'll make sure you're rewarded.'

'Ah well, I suppose that's all right, then,' said Sancho, with a sigh. 'I mean, I'm happy to help out. I'd just rather not be doing it for nothing.'

As they stopped to have some food a boy came along the road.

'You!' the boy exclaimed, and Don Quixote recognized the boy he'd rescued from being hit by his master.

'You know what you did, don't you?' said the boy, accusingly. 'You made my master so furious he gave me the sack.'

'Then by my oath as a knight-errant—' began Don Quixote, exceedingly angry.

'Oh no,' said the boy. 'No, I've had enough of that. Look, mister, if you see me in trouble again, just ignore me, all right? Because however bad things are, I reckon you're pretty much bound to make them even worse.'

Towards evening they reached Sancho's blanket-flipping inn once again, and after Don Quixote had promised to pay his bill, the innkeeper let them in. Don Quixote went to bed at once, exhausted, but the others sat up and discussed his strange ways.

'In some ways I can understand it,' said the innkeeper. 'I have three books of knightly tales myself, and when we have a guest who can read, we all crowd round and thoroughly enjoy them. The way Don Cirongilio of Thrace strangles that dragon! I wish I'd been there to see it.'

'My dear innkeeper,' said the priest, 'none of those tales are true.'

'What? When the books have been licensed by the king? Of course they are – though of course none of that stuff happens nowadays.'

The news that knightly adventure was a thing of the past worried Sancho a great deal, and he was wondering whether he should go back to farming when the priest began to read them a story from one of the innkeeper's books. That soon made Sancho forgot all about reality.

The priest hadn't got very far when there was a huge commotion overhead.

'Take that, scoundrel!' roared Don Quixote. 'I have you at last! Your scimitar shall not save you!'

'Look at the stairs!' gasped Sancho. 'A river of blood! Don Quixote must be fighting a giant! *Quick!*'

They charged upstairs and found Don Quixote, his nightcap on and eyes tightly closed, slashing away wildly with his sword. He'd already smashed a huge jar of pomegranate juice, which was what had caused the flood on the stairs.

The innkeeper was so angry, he rushed over and punched Don Quixote on the nose, but the Knight of the Sad Face didn't wake up until the barber threw a bucket of water over him.

'Princess!' gasped Don Quixote, still only half awake. 'I have killed the evil Giant Pandafilando! You are free!'

'You have?' said Sancho, searching all the corners of the room. 'Well, he must be enchanted, then, because *I* can't find him.'

'Never mind enchantments,' shouted the innkeeper. 'What about my jar?'

'Huh,' said Sancho, very aggrieved. 'You think you've got troubles. Now Don Quixote's killed the giant we won't have to visit the princess's kingdom, will we, and that means I've probably just lost a governorship.'

The princess comforted Sancho by telling him that as soon as she had her kingdom, he should have his governorship.

Soon Don Quixote fell asleep again, so the priest finished reading them the story from the innkeeper's book, which, most satisfactorily, ended up with more or less all the guilty parties (which was everyone) dropping dead.

The priest had just closed the pages of the book when four men and a woman, all on fine horses and wearing travelling masks, arrived at the inn. The lady sat down at once and heaved a sigh so piteous that Dorotea asked if there was anything she could do to help.

'Don't waste your sympathy, she'll only tell you lies,' said one of the travellers, quickly; but at this the masked woman burst out: 'I have never lied! Indeed, it is my truthfulness which brings me to such misery.'

Cardenio sat up at the sound of her voice.

'It's you!' he said. 'Luscinda!'

The masked lady at once tried to turn to him, but the

man who'd spoken grabbed her arm, and in the struggle their masks fell off.

Dorotea gazed at the man, turned slowly white, gasped one single word: '*Fernando!*' and fainted into the barber's arms.

Fernando was struck rigid with astonishment.

'Don Fernando,' said Luscinda, recovering her powers of speech. 'You must know by now that no threats or violence can ever make me forget Cardenio, my one true love. So let me go to him.'

Dorotea disentangled herself from the barber and threw herself at Fernando's feet.

'Fernando, you gave me your word that I am your wife,' she said. 'You cannot deny me if you are a gentleman!'

By now everyone was sobbing, even Fernando's servants (though Sancho said afterwards that he was only crying because he'd realized that Dorotea wasn't really a princess and so didn't have any governorships to give away).

At last Fernando let Luscinda go, saying, 'Loveliest Dorotea. No one could deny such truth. You have saved my good name and my good character.'

Then Luscinda fainted briefly into Cardenio's arms, and everyone cried so much you would have thought some great disaster had come upon them instead of two happy endings.

Eventually everyone stopped weeping (including the innkeeper, because Cardenio promised to pay for all the damage Don Quixote had done on his visits) except for poor Sancho, who went to bed still mourning his lost governorship.

'The only trouble is, now that Dorotea's no longer the Princess Micomicona, how on earth are we going to get Don Quixote home?' asked the priest.

Don Fernando scratched his beard.

'Perhaps Dorotea had better carry on being the princess for now,' he said. 'Don Quixote brought us together, and so we owe it to him to see him safely home.'

Just then, Don Quixote came downstairs, followed by an anxious Sancho, and told the princess that although he'd killed the giant Pandafilando (which he had, in his dreams), he thought he'd still better accompany her home to make sure she got her kingdom back. The princess accepted this offer in the best of spirits.

By that time Sancho was very confused indeed, but in the end he decided that Dorotea must somehow be a princess, after all.

So then he cheered up, too.

Just as they were going to bed (all except for Don Quixote, who insisted on doing guard duty outside the 'castle' all night), a judge and his young daughter Doña Clara arrived at the inn, which was by this time so full that

Doña Clara had to share Dorotea and Luscinda's room.

Now, it so happened that there was a hatch high up in the outside wall of the inn for taking in straw, and this gave the innkeeper's daughter an idea for a joke. She went to the hatch, from where she could see Don Quixote on guard duty, and called his name through the grille that covered it.

Of course Don Quixote decided at once that the young woman was trying to chat him up.

'Dear lady,' he said. 'I fear I cannot love you as your beauty deserves. My heart is another's.'

'I'm not after your heart,' she said.

'Then how can I help you?'

'Just give me your hand, sir.'

So Don Quixote manoeuvred Rocinante under the hatch and stood up precariously on his saddle. And as soon as Don Quixote put his hand up to the hatch, the innkeeper's daughter slipped the one end of a rope round his wrist, tied the other end to the hayloft door, and then ran away laughing.

Poor Don Quixote was left balanced on Rocinante's saddle, sure he was the victim of an enchanter, and terrified that Rocinante would walk off and leave him dangling.

Meanwhile, on the other side of the inn, someone was singing the loveliest love song in the world outside

Dorotea and Luscinda's room. They couldn't think who it could be, until Doña Clara flushed deep red and gave the game away. The singer was Don Luis, a boy of Doña Clara's own age. He loved her passionately, but he was too high-born to ask for her hand in marriage.

Dorotea and Luscinda naturally found the whole affair completely thrilling.

Chapter Seven

The next morning at dawn, some new guests coming up the road woke up Rocinante, who sidestepped a little and made Don Quixote slip off his saddle. Soon everyone in the inn was startled awake by Don Quixote's screams. Well, everyone rushed down to see what was happening, but the innkeeper's daughter got there first, undid the rope, and all everyone found when they arrived was Don Quixote, collapsed and groaning on the ground.

Don Quixote, very confused, immediately challenged the new arrivals to a fight, but luckily they took no notice because they were busy looking for a young man called Don Luis, who was known to have been following Doña Clara's carriage.

They soon found him, fast asleep and disguised as a footman, but otherwise their quest ended in failure because when they woke Don Luis up, he proclaimed his desperate love for Doña Clara and flatly refused to go home.

At this point, as if things weren't complicated enough, the innkeeper caught two men trying to sneak out of the inn without paying, and before you could say 'knight errant' they were all fighting hammer and tongs. The innkeeper's wife ran to Don Quixote and begged him for help, but of course Don Quixote only fought men of high birth, so all he could do was reason with them.

Meanwhile, Doña Clara's father, the judge, was in a fix. The young lovers were clearly crazy about each other, and Don Luis would make a nice rich husband for his daughter – but it would be madness to go against the wishes of Don Luis's father.

It wasn't long before Don Quixote's reasoning had so completely freaked out the men fighting the innkeeper that they paid their bill in full just to get away from him. Things might have calmed down a bit then, if the barber from whom Don Quixote and Sancho had stolen the helm of Mambrino hadn't rolled up, shouted, 'Give me back my basin!' at Sancho, and started to beat *him* up.

Don Quixote was delighted with the fierce way Sancho defended himself.

'We won it fairly,' Don Quixote explained, once Sancho and the barber had been separated. 'What this man calls a basin is actually the famous helmet of Mambrino. Go and get it, Sancho, and show everyone.'

'Are you sure?' said Sancho. But he went and got it.

'Now, what sort of a fool would call *this* a basin?' asked Don Quixote, when it came.

'Oh, a *real* fool,' said Don Quixote's barber-from-home, who was enjoying the whole scene immensely, and Don Fernando and Cardenio backed him up.

'I suppose you'll say the saddle he stole wasn't a saddle,

either?' demanded the Mambrino's-helm barber, furiously.

'Well, it's never easy to be sure when there are enchanters involved,' said Don Quixote.

'Let's vote on it,' said Don Fernando happily, and he went round asking everyone their opinion. Everyone who knew Don Quixote found this hilarious, but Don Luis's servants, and some King's guards who'd just arrived, thought the whole thing utter nonsense, especially when Don Fernando announced the result of the vote, which was that the saddle wasn't a saddle at all.

'Anyone who thinks that's not a saddle doesn't know what he's talking about!' said one of the King's guards, upon which Don Quixote promptly gave him a jab with his pike.

So of course then the other King's guards piled in to help their friend, and Sancho and the basin barber started a tug-of-war with the saddle with Don Fernando and Cardenio joining in on one side, and the innkeeper joining in on the other. Suddenly the courtyard was all fists, shouting, cudgels, pounding, shrieking, weeping and fainting.

Into all this chaos Don Quixote shouted, with a voice of thunder, 'Stop, if you value your lives!'

And suddenly everyone did.

'My dear friends,' said Don Quixote, with great dignity. 'With all these enchantments everywhere, how can fighting solve anything?'

And as the fight had resulted in the saddle being torn almost in two, everybody had to agree.

So everyone forgave each other (even the King's guards forgave people once they'd discovered how important Don Fernando was) and then, as Don Luis was still loudly determined not to return home, Don Fernando soothed away that problem by inviting Don Luis to stay at his castle.

Everything would have been lovely, then, if one of the guards hadn't gone and remembered he was searching for a tall thin madman who'd set a load of convicts free. Well, the guard seized Don Quixote by the collar – and Don Quixote seized *him* by the throat – and all the row might have started again if Don Fernando hadn't separated them.

'Don't you know the law cannot touch a knight errant?' demanded Don Quixote, angrily.

'Look,' said the priest quietly to the guards. 'If you arrest him they'll only let him go again because he obviously doesn't know what he's doing.'

'Not my problem,' said an officer. 'I just have to nab them.'

But Don Quixote continued to act so oddly, addressing Dorotea as 'Princess' and urging her to leave the castle before enchantments caused any more trouble, that in

the end the officers had to admit that Don Quixote was
addle-pated and they agreed to let the matter drop.
Then Sancho and the basin barber agreed to
swap saddles, the priest secretly gave the
basin-barber some money for Mambrino's helm,
and Don Fernando paid for everything else.

By this time everyone had had quite enough
of Don Quixote, so the King's guards and Don
Quixote's friends the barber and the priest put
their heads together and came up with a plan.
They made themselves some monster masks and
when Don Quixote was resting they jumped on
him, tied him up, put him in a cage on an ox cart,
and told him that he was temporarily enchanted
but would soon be with Dulcinea.

Don Quixote took this news quite happily, and promised Sancho that, even if he didn't get a governorship, Don Quixote would definitely pay him some wages when they got home.

The ox cart creaked off on its way escorted by the guards, the priest and the barber, all in their monster masks, and all went well until some travellers caught up with the cart and, understandably enough, asked what on earth was going on.

'Er ... it's an enchantment,' said the priest, weakly.

But Sancho said, 'Oh, how can you say such a thing, Reverend, and you a priest? You know full well that my master's not enchanted. Why, if you hadn't tied him up he might be married to a princess by now, and I'd be a governor. Don't you feel sorry for doing down my wife and children like that, and for all the poor folk Don Quixote isn't helping because you've put him in a cage?'

The priest hurriedly took the travellers aside and explained everything, but while they were talking, Sancho crept up to Don Quixote's cage.

'Those aren't really monsters,' he whispered, 'they're the priest and the barber and some King's guards. Look, answer me one question and I'll prove it.'

'You can't prove anything with enchantments, Sancho.'

'You can with this. Tell me: *do you want to go to the toilet?*'

'Er ... well, I have been tied up for some time ... '

'There! That proves it! Because think about it: in all those old stories *no one enchanted ever does*!'

It was a good point, though unfortunately Don Quixote still couldn't bring himself to believe it. Still, once he'd promised not to run away, they let him out of his cage so he could go off and make himself comfortable.

'You know that all those knightly stories are just made up, don't you?' said one of the travellers, when Don Quixote returned.

'Of course they're not,' retorted Don Quixote. 'El Cid – King Arthur – they're real, and inspiring, and beautiful! Why, just think of all the good I've done since I've been a knight errant.'

'I wish you'd done a bit more, and could have made me a governor,' said Sancho, wistfully.

Don Quixote was about to climb back into his cage when some men carrying a statue came round the corner.

'Good heavens!' exclaimed Don Quixote. 'A captive lady!' He jumped on Rocinante and before they could stop him he charged to the rescue.

No one was to blame for what happened next. One of the men escorting the statue ran forward to meet the attack, dodged Don Quixote's sword, and gave

Don Quixote such a blow with his stick that the Knight of the Sad Face was knocked flying. He rolled over and over and then lay, motionless.

Sancho ran to him, crying, convinced his master was dead.

Eventually, Don Quixote stirred.

'I think this enchantment has affected my fighting skills, Sancho,' he whispered, weakly. 'Perhaps I'd better go home until it's worn off.'

'And then we'll try again,' said Sancho, comfortingly.

It was obvious that Don Quixote was too battered to cause any more trouble, so the King's guards decided to leave the others to journey home alone. They helped Don Quixote back into the cage, and six days later the barber, the priest, Sancho and Don Quixote arrived back at the village.

The first thing Sancho's wife Teresa did was to ask after the donkey, and after that she asked about presents.

'I haven't brought any presents, exactly,' said Sancho. 'But I'll be sure to bring some next time, just you wait and see. Being a squire is the best life in the world!'

'Watch him carefully,' said the priest to Don Quixote's niece. 'Because if you don't, he'll be off again.'

And that is exactly what happened, although the only account I have of Don Quixote's further adventures comes from some verses I found in an old casket.

Don Quixote's in his grave.
No knight so true, or mad, or brave.

No maid was so loved as the moon-faced Dulcinea;
Than poor Don Quixote, no boyfriend was skinnier.

Here lies poor Sancho, out of luck.
Although a fool, he had some pluck.

All I ask now is that you believe this history, so carefully assembled, in exactly the same way that you believe all those other tales of glorious knight-errantry.

And now all we can do is to hope that at some point, we get news of some more of Don Quixote's adventures.

VOLUME TWO

Dear Reader,

If you've read that terrible book that some fool's brought out recently, the one that claims to be a second book of stories about Don Quixote, then I feel sorry for you, because it's absolutely dreadful.

That awful book was not only written without my permission, but practically everything in it is wrong.

The important thing is that it's this book, here, which is the true sequel to Don Quixote*: it was written by me, Cervantes, and it finishes Don Quixote's story in the proper way.*

I must thank the great Count of Lemos and the Archbishop of Toledo, who have protected and helped me, and saved me from poverty.

I must also mention that I, Cervantes, have some more books in the pipeline, so I hope you'll look out for them, too.

Miguel de Cervantes

Chapter One

Don Quixote's friends, the barber and the priest, hoped very much that time would make Don Quixote forget his knight-errantry nonsense, and so they left him alone for several weeks. When they did finally go to see Don Quixote, he seemed so sane and wise that they were overjoyed.

Then the priest went and mentioned the possibility of Spain being invaded, and everything went horribly wrong.

'The King should send for his knights errant,' said Don Quixote. 'Half a dozen of them could wipe out a hundred thousand of the enemy!'

'You're not starting that knight errant thing again!' said Don Quixote's niece, in dismay.

'Starting it *again*?' he echoed. 'I've never *stopped* being a knight errant, niece, and I'll be one till I die. Who else shall protect the weak? Knights nowadays may go around decked out in silk, but there's not one who could fight a giant. Who's as brave nowadays as Amadis, or as invincible as Roland?'

'But my friend, they weren't real people,' said the priest.

'No, no, they are as true as I am! Amadis, for example, was a tall man with a black beard.'

'I see,' said the barber. 'And ... how about giants?'

'Ah, giants. Well, they weren't nearly as big as you'd think, for in the stories they often slept in houses,' said Don Quixote.

At this point there was a commotion outside and Sancho arrived with a man called Sansón who had just finished his studies at the university.

'Be off with you, Sancho!' said the housekeeper. 'We don't want you coming in here and leading our master astray again!'

'But it's *him* that led *me* astray,' protested Sancho. 'And he promised me an isle I never got!'

'An isle? What's that? Something to put in your great fat belly?'

'My dear Sancho,' said Don Quixote, happily. 'Come in, come in.'

The barber and the priest left the house, shaking their heads.

'He'll be off on his adventures again,' said the priest. 'And Sancho's stupid enough to go with him, too.'

'Now,' said Don Quixote, to Sancho and Sansón, once the priest and the barber had gone. 'What are people saying about me, Sancho?'

'Well, some say you're a lunatic, some say you're above yourself, and some say you're funny.'

'I'm not surprised. Goodness is generally rewarded like that. They said Amadis was a cry-baby, you know.'

'I know, but guess what? Our adventures have been put into a book, just like Amadis's were. Sansón here, he's from the university, he's read it. It's called *Don Quixote,* but me and Dulcinea are in it and everything.'

'Good heavens. Can this be true?'

'Oh yes,' said Sansón, throwing himself to his knees and clasping Don Quixote's hands. 'You are famous throughout Europe, great Don Quixote.'

'And it's all in there?'

'Yes, fights and blanket-flippings and windmills and all. In fact, some people say they wish there wasn't so much in it about your being beaten up.'

'Hm. No, they needn't have put all that in.'

'But as a true history it *must* go in, sir. In any case, other people complain much more about Sancho being stupid enough to believe he'd get to govern his isle; and others moan about all the lovey-dovey stuff. But people still love the book.'

'The writer must be a real genius, then,' said Don Quixote.

'Yes, even though people *will* find fault – like the fact that it doesn't say what Sancho did with the money he found in the Sierra Morena.'

'I spent it on the family, of course,' said Sancho. 'Coo, if I'd come home empty-handed I'd have been for it!'

'And does the author promise a second part?' asked Don Quixote.

'Yes, he does, once he's found an account of some more adventures. Mind you, some people are saying that sequels are never as good as the original, and others are saying they've had quite enough of you already.'

'You wait,' said Sancho. 'By the time we've finished there'll be so many adventures they'll hardly fit in a library.'

'Indeed,' said Don Quixote. 'We must set out at once for ... '

'How about the jousting in Saragossa?' suggested Sancho. 'Winning there would make you dead famous.'

' ... Saragossa without delay.'

'And then I'll get my isle to govern,' said Sancho, very pleased. 'Oh, but there's just one thing, Master, I'm not doing any more fighting. I'll be the most loyal squire ever, but I'm not cut out to be a hero, me.'

Sancho rushed home to his wife Teresa.

'I'm going to be a governor, and our daughter Sanchita will marry an earl!' he cried.

Teresa sniffed.

'I think Sanchita and I will be much happier staying as we are, thank you,' she said.

'But you're old!' said Don Quixote's niece, when she

heard about his plan.

'Can't you just be a knight at court, Master?' asked his housekeeper.

'My dearly-beloved nitwits, the only two ways to get riches and honour are through letters and bravery. And it's bravery – which naturally includes kindness and generosity – for me.'

The housekeeper rushed away to Sansón.

'Tell my master not to go away!' she begged. 'It cost us a hundred eggs to get him back on his feet after last time, as my hens will tell you.'

When they arrived at Don Quixote's house, they found Sancho asking for some regular wages.

'Oh, my dear Sancho,' said Don Quixote. 'If you need wages then I'm afraid I'm going to have to go without you. No squire in any of the stories gets wages, you know.'

'Oh, no, I'll come, I'll come,' said Sancho, tears coming to his eyes at the thought of being left behind. 'I only asked for wages because Teresa made me. But there, a man must be a man.'

And so Don Quixote and Sancho Panza rode out once again on their adventures, and all Sansón could do was to wave them goodbye.

Chapter Two

'First we will go and pay homage to the great lady Dulcinea at Toboso,' said Don Quixote. 'And then we'll carry on our fight against evil.'

'Couldn't we do that just by being extra good?' asked Sancho, but Don Quixote took no notice.

They arrived at Toboso at midnight.

'Lead the way to Dulcinea's castle, Sancho,' ordered Don Quixote.

Well, that was a problem because, despite what he'd told Don Quixote, Sancho had never been to Dulcinea's house in his life.

'Find it in the dark?' Sancho asked. 'Can't *you* find it? You must have been here loads of times.'

'Of course I haven't, you fool! I only know Dulcinea through the rumours I've heard of her beauty and intelligence.'

'Really? Well, all right, then, you know that time I met her? *That* was only rumours, as well.'

'This is no time for joking, Sancho!'

'All right. But look, we can't go enquiring after Dulcinea in the middle of the night: think what that'd do to her reputation. I'll tell you what, you go and hide out somewhere. I'll do some investigating, and arrange a meeting place for you both.'

'Very well,' said Don Quixote, turning away towards the nearest wood. 'But watch her carefully when you tell her I'm here. See if she blushes.'

'So,' said Sancho to himself, as Rocinante clopped away. 'I'm trying to find a castle in a small village, and if people find me chatting up one of their women they'll beat me black and blue. I must be as muddled as Don Quixote, who confuses giants and windmills ... hey, hang on ... if he's *that* mad he'll believe anything.'

Sancho waited until he saw three peasant girls coming along on donkeys, and then he hastened to Don Quixote, whom he found happily singing love songs.

'Dulcinea's coming, Master, with two of her maids! Look! All covered in diamonds, and riding a gannet!'

'But those are peasant girls on donkeys, Sancho,' said Don Quixote. 'And it's jennet, not gannet.' [6]

'Peasants? Donkeys? Your eyes must be enchanted, Master.'

Sancho ran to kneel in front of one of the girls' donkeys, calling her 'beautiful princess', and Don Quixote, very confused, went and knelt beside him.

'Get lost,' said the girl.

---

[6] A jennet is a fine horse. A gannet looks like a big seagull.

'Be gentle, I pray you … er … peerless beauty,' said Don Quixote, squinting doubtfully up at her.

'Ooh, hark at grandad,' said the girl. 'Now get out of the way.'

Sancho obeyed, delighted to have got out of this tricky problem so easily, and the girls cantered briskly round Don Quixote and away down the road.

Sancho and Don Quixote rode on towards Saragossa, Don Quixote lamenting as they went the evil enchantment that had been cast over his eyes and nose. The beautiful Dulcinea had appeared flat-nosed to him, and scented with finest garlic.

Don Quixote and Sancho rode on past nightfall, talking as they went.

'I think you're growing less foolish, dear Sancho,' said Don Quixote.

'Well, I'm bound to, spending so much time with you,' said Sancho. 'My mind was just poor barren soil, before, but you're the manure that's making it bear fruit.'

They stopped at last and slept under some trees, and Rocinante and the donkey stood together as such good friends do.

It was still pitch dark when Don Quixote was woken by the clattering of hooves and then some clanking, as if a knight in armour had dismounted and thrown himself on the ground.

'We will let the horses rest while I think thoughts of love,' said a voice.

Don Quixote crawled over in great excitement and woke up Sancho.

'He must be another knight errant,' said Don Quixote. 'Listen, he's tuning some musical instrument. I think he's going to sing!'

And he did.

> *'You bid me ride away,*
> *So, Lady, I obey,*
> *My will is all your own,*
> *Though duty makes me groan,*

'Oh Casildea,' the man went on. 'Why will you have me waste away in cruel labours? Is it not enough that all the knights of Spain acknowledge your peerless beauty?'

'What?' said Don Quixote, sitting up. 'Who says? *I* don't acknowledge it.'

'Who goes there?' said the singer, sharply. 'A happy man, or one sorrowful?'

'One sorrowful.'

It turned out that the man was indeed another love-lorn knight errant. Sancho left them to sigh together and went off with the singing knight's squire to have a good chat.

'It's not an easy life, is it?' said the singing knight's squire.

'It's certainly a hungry one,' said Sancho. 'Sometimes you can travel a whole day on nothing more than the wind that blows in your face.'

'Still, there's always the chance of being made a bishop.'

'Oh, I hope not. I'd make an awful bishop. I'm hoping to be the governor of an isle.'

'Yes, but even isles aren't what they used to be,' said the squire, gloomily. 'To be honest I've almost decided to jack in this squiring lark. I mean, my Master's looking for some mad knight errant, and goodness knows what'll happen when we find him. My knight's brave enough, but he's not that clever – and he's villainous, too.'

'Oh, mine's not villainous,' said Sancho. 'He lives to help people. That's the trouble, really: I love him so much I can't bear to leave him.'

'She's beautiful, is Casildea,' said the singing knight to Don Quixote, 'but she will keep sending me on quests. You name it, I've had to do it: sorting out giantesses, jumping down chasms ... though the bravest thing I've ever done is to get Don Quixote, the greatest knight in Spain, to admit that Casildea is more beautiful than his Dulcinea.'

'Don Quixote admitted that?' asked Don Quixote. 'Are you *sure* it was him?'

'Oh yes, there can't be two like that: skinny, wrinkly,

drooping moustache.'

'But *I* am Don Quixote!' said Don Quixote. 'My friend, some enchanter must have been impersonating me. But never mind, we can still fight each other.'

The singing knight stood up.

'I shall be ready at sunrise,' he said, and they both went off to tell their squires to prepare for battle.

'I'll be sorry to hurt you,' said the singing knight's squire to Sancho.

'Hurt *me*?' said Sancho. 'But I'm not fighting. I haven't got a sword.'

'Well, I've got a couple of pillows. We could have a pillow fight.'

'A pillow fight?'

'Yes. We'll put some rocks in them, and—'

'Oh no, you can forget that. Anyway, I have to be angry to fight.'

'I could sneak up behind you and wallop you. That'd make you angry.'

'You do that and I'll bash you so hard you'll never hit anyone again!'

Dawn came at last, and Don Quixote and Sancho saw the singing knight and his squire clearly for the first time. The squire looked so ferocious, with a nose exactly like an aubergine, that Sancho, trembling, retreated quietly up a tree.

The singing knight had plumes on his helmet, a steel-tipped lance, a surcoat sparkling with sequins, and his visor down.

'Ready to fight?' he said, grasping his lance.

'Ready,' said Don Quixote.

'And the loser shall obey the orders of the winner?'

'Agreed,' said Don Quixote.

The singing knight had the best armour, but unfortunately his horse was ancient. After a few yards of mild trotting, it stumbled to a halt, while Rocinante, suddenly taking it into his head to gallop for the first time in his life, brought Don Quixote thundering down on the knight in the sequins and knocked him flying.

Don Quixote quickly dismounted, took off the knight's helmet ... and there, before his eyes, was Sansón the university man.

Sancho couldn't believe it. 'Kill him straight away!' he shouted. 'He must be an enchanter!'

'No, no!' said his squire, running up. 'It's really him!'

Sancho stared at the squire in astonishment.

'Where's your nose gone?'

'It's here, in my pocket.'

Sancho stared some more. 'Tomé! You're my friend Tomé from home!'

Meanwhile the knight in the sequins was waking up to find Don Quixote's sword at his throat. He quickly agreed to go to Toboso and tell Dulcinea she was the fairest lady in Spain, and very soon he was riding painfully away, defeated, his squire beside him.

Sancho was completely baffled by the whole incident, but Don Quixote, speaking wisely of enchantments, explained that a man could never believe the evidence of his own eyes.

'Think how that enchantment made Dulcinea seem to me like a garlic-breathed peasant,' he said.

Sancho couldn't argue with that.

'So, that plan you cooked up with the priest and the barber didn't work too well, did it, Sansón?' said Tomé, as they rode along.

'I'd have beaten Don Quixote easily if I'd had a better horse,' said Sansón, crossly. 'And then I could have ordered him to go home where he's safe.'

'You really think you'd have beaten him?'

'Of course I do,' said Sansón. 'And next time I *will*, too.'

Chapter Three

Don Quixote and Sancho packed up and set off, and they hadn't been travelling long before a gentleman caught up with them. Don Diego naturally took Don Quixote for an imbecile to start with, but the Knight of the Sad Face spoke so sensibly about the beauty and truth that is revealed by literature, that by the time they saw a cart decked with royal banners coming towards them, Don Diego had decided that Don Quixote wasn't quite such a fool as he'd thought.

He soon changed his mind again, for at once Don Quixote put on his helmet, discovered that Sancho had been using it to store yogurt, wiped his face, and then demanded to be told what the cart was carrying.

'A pair of lions, as presents to the King,' said the carter.

'Excellent!' said Don Quixote. 'Open their cage so I can fight them.'

Well, Sancho, Don Diego and the carter begged Don Quixote to leave the lions alone, but Don Quixote lowered his lance threateningly and in the end all they could do was ride away as far as they could – all except for the carter, whom Don Quixote forced to open the lions' crate.

The lions yawned, showing their terrible teeth, as the door opened. Then they stretched their great limbs ...

... and then they went back to sleep again.

'Great heavens!' exclaimed the carter, hastily. 'Your bravery and ferocity has tamed the beasts! Hurrah for knights errant!'

And he swiftly closed the crate door again.

It took a while to persuade the others to return, but when they did, Don Quixote declared himself 'Knight of the Lions,' and then he, Sancho and Don Diego rode on together until they came to Don Diego's house, where he'd invited them to stay.

Don Quixote washed the yogurt out of his hair with five (or possibly six; accounts vary) buckets of water, and went down to where Don Diego's son, Don Lorenzo, was waiting to recite them some poetry.

'I am a student of knight-errantry, Don Lorenzo, as you are of poetry,' said Don Quixote.

'I didn't know knight-errantry was studied.'

'Oh yes. A knight errant must be judge, lawyer, doctor, navigator, smith and mathematician. He must also study compassion and truth.'

'Then it is indeed a great study,' said Don Lorenzo, politely.

They stayed four or five days at Don Diego's house, eating and resting and listening to Don Lorenzo's poetry:

*'This cruel life
Is death's disguise:
But then to die
Is no great prize.'*

But soon Don Quixote decided they must be on their way. A knight errant is always on the move, and in any case he fancied a trip down the famous cave of Montesinos, which wasn't far away.

They soon fell in with some students who were bound for the wedding of Quiteria the fair and Camacho the rich. It was going to be a big do, everyone invited, and the only slight problem might be if a man called Basilio turned up, because he was so desperately in love with Quiteria that he'd gone really weird since the wedding was announced.

'I wish people could choose who to marry,' said Sancho.

'Oh no,' said Don Quixote. 'Love blinds the understanding, and on a long journey you need a trustworthy companion.'

'Well, we're afraid that Basilio *will* end his journey the moment Quiteria says "I will",' said one of the students. 'We're almost sure he'll die of grief on the spot.'

The place where the wedding was going to take place proved to be full of busy preparations and the scent of good food.

Don Quixote, much to Sancho's disgust, insisted on

spending the night in a field under the many shining stars.

Don Quixote woke early, before the sun had dried the pearls of the dew. Sancho was still sleeping, but Don Quixote poked him awake with his lance.

Sancho sat up and sniffed.

'Someone's cooking meat,' he said. 'Brilliant! Hey, you can't really blame a girl for going for a rich guy, can you?'

The wedding field was filled with music and enormous amounts of food. One of the cooks gave Sancho a huge saucepan full of boiled geese and told him to keep the saucepan.

Meanwhile, troupes of young dancers were busy everywhere. Don Quixote would have enjoyed it all thoroughly if Sancho, chewing away, hadn't kept up a running commentary the whole time.

'Sancho, I hope to see you struck dumb before I die,' said Don Quixote, wearily, at last.

'The way you work me, I may drop dead tomorrow,' retorted Sancho.

The bride proved to be the loveliest of women (except for Dulcinea), though she was rather pale. She made her way to the platform where the ceremony was going to take place, but as she mounted the steps there was some frenzied shouting and a man in black appeared.

'Quiteria!' he shouted. 'You promised to marry *me,* remember? Me, Basilio. That means you can't honestly marry anyone else. But never fear, Quiteria: I shall take that obstacle out of your way.'

And suddenly he drew his sword and stabbed himself, so that the point of the blade protruded from his back.

He fell down, bleeding freely.

'I'm ... dying,' he gasped. 'Quiteria! Marry me while I yet live, and then I can die content. It will be only for an instant.'

Quiteria went paler than ever, but she went to kneel beside him and vowed that she married him of her own free will. He just about managed to gasp out the words of the rest of the ceremony.

The moment the marriage ceremony was complete, Basilio sprang to his feet and tore away the tube of blood into which he'd plunged his sword to give the effect of a fatal wound.

At once a hubbub broke out.

'That marriage doesn't count!' shouted someone. 'It was based on a trick!'

But it hadn't been based on a trick at all, for Quiteria confessed that she'd known all about Basilio's plan. At this, Camacho and his men drew their swords, and Basilio's friends drew theirs, and there would have been much blood spilled if Don Quixote hadn't ridden Rocinante between the two sides, shouting that all was fair in love and war.

'You are still rich, Camacho,' he shouted. 'You still have treasures galore: Basilio has only Quiteria!'

And when Camacho came to think about it, he realized that marrying a woman who loved someone else would probably have caused endless trouble, so he decided that on the whole he'd got off lightly. So Camacho stayed to eat his feast, and Basilio and Quiteria, with Don Quixote and Sancho, rode off home to their village.

The only one who was heartbroken was Sancho, because he missed the rest of the feast.

Don Quixote stayed with the newly-weds for three days and gave them much advice about a virtuous wife being the secret to happiness.

'I wish someone had told *me* that before I got married,' said Sancho.

'But surely Teresa is virtuous, Sancho.'

'Not always.'

'Oh, Sancho, Sancho ... you should always speak well of the mother of your children.'

'Oh, no, it's all right. She says just the same about me.'

At last Don Quixote and Sancho set out for the famous Cave of Montesinos. Don Quixote hacked away the crow-filled bushes round the mouth of the cave, and then Sancho lowered him into the darkness. Sancho lowered him the whole length of the rope, which was two hundred metres, and then, after about half an hour, he pulled him back up again only to find Don Quixote dangling limply on the rope, unconscious. Sancho dragged Don Quixote up onto firm ground and shook him frantically, sobbing with fear.

At last Don Quixote opened his eyes.

'I thought you'd died in that awful place!' cried Sancho.

'Awful place? Oh no, it wasn't awful. You sit down, and I'll tell you all about it.'

'I was nearly at the bottom of the cave,' said Don Quixote, 'when I saw a ledge. Well, I sat down on it and I think I must have fallen asleep, for when I awoke, there before my eyes was an old man and a castle made of crystal.

'"Welcome, valiant Don Quixote!" the old man said.

'Well, it turned out that the old man was Montesinos himself, so of course I asked him if it was true he'd cut out the heart of his dead friend Durandarte with a dagger and taken it to the Lady Belerma. And he said it was all quite true, except that it hadn't been a dagger, but a penknife.

'We went into the castle, and there was the corpse of poor Durandarte. The oddest thing was that although he was dead, Durandarte still occasionally recited bits of verse:

*'"When from this sad life I part
Let Belerma keep my heart."*

'Well, Montesinos told me that Merlin had imprisoned everyone from Durandarte story there (except for Durandarte's squire, whom he'd turned into a river, and some ladies-in-waiting, who are now lakes).

'"Don't worry, Durandarte," Montesinos said to the corpse. "Don Quixote will help us!"

'At that point a woman in black (who was of course Belerma) arrived carrying a shrivelled heart. Her nose was rather snout-like, and she had dark rings under her eyes, but Montesinos explained that this was because of her great grief at Durandarte's death.'

'Hmm,' said Sancho, dubiously. 'Are you sure about all this, Master?'

'Yes, yes. Why, I even saw the lovely Dulcinea and her companions.'

'Right,' said Sancho. 'So ... how did you recognize them?'

'Well, because one of her companions asked me if Dulcinea could borrow a bit of cash.'

'That there Montesinos's stolen your wits,' said Sancho.

'But I haven't told you half of it,' cried Don Quixote, even though he was himself wondering if he'd dreamed the whole thing.

Don Quixote and Sancho soon set off once more, and at last they came to a place even Don Quixote recognized as an inn, and not a castle. There was a man there with a load of weapons and it turned out that the weapons were destined to settle a very odd argument.

The trouble had started when a man's donkey got lost. Luckily, a neighbour had spotted the beast going into the trees, so he and the donkey's owner split up and began to search the forest. Well, they searched for ages, and in the end, all the donkey's owner could think to do was to bray as loud as he could in the hope the donkey would reply – and, sure enough, straight away there was a bray in answer.

Well, he brayed again, and then he brayed some more, and in the end he found …

… his neighbour. Because it turned out that the neighbour was brilliant at braying, too.

The poor donkey turned out to have been eaten by wolves.

'All the other villages are making terrible fun of us,' said the man with the load of weapons, disgustedly. 'So now we're going to fight them, and these weapons are to protect us.'

At that point, a man with an eyepatch arrived at the inn. He was called Pedro, and he had a magic ape that could answer questions.

'Can he really?' said Sancho. 'All right. What's my wife doing?'

The ape jumped up on Pedro's shoulder and chattered

in his ear.

Pedro threw up his hands in astonishment.

'This is the mighty Don Quixote!' he exclaimed. 'And this is Sancho Panza. Señor Panza, your wife is currently drinking chocolate and spinning flax!'

'That does sound like Teresa,' admitted Sancho.

Everyone was amazed, especially Don Quixote.[7]

'And now,' announced Pedro, 'for the great Don Quixote, I will perform my magnificent puppet show!'

And the puppet show was magnificent, right up until the point where the puppet army came along to separate the doomed puppet lovers. Unfortunately, then Don Quixote got overexcited. He drew his sword and chopped the whole papier mâché horde into a thousand pieces.

Luckily by the time everyone had come out from under the tables, Don Quixote had quietened down and agreed to pay Pedro for the damage.

The next morning they all went on their different ways. Pedro left very early; it was almost as if he didn't want to risk seeing Don Quixote ever again.

---

[7] Those who don't believe in magic apes may be a feeling doubtful about the truth of the adventure at the inn, but the reason the eyepatched Pedro recognized Don Quixote was because he was really none other than that dreadful villain Ginés, the chained convict.

Chapter Four

Don Quixote and Sancho had been riding for a while when they saw a banner with a donkey on it, and they realized that the battle of the braying villagers was about to begin.

The villagers were about two hundred strong. Don Quixote at once addressed them.

'My dear sirs,' he said. 'Do think again. Jokes aren't a good reason for fighting.'

'That's right!' said Sancho. 'I mean, when I was young I used to be good at braying, too, like this – '

And holding his nose he let out such a loud and realistic bray that a man, convinced Sancho was mocking him, gave Sancho a furious blow that knocked him out.

Don Quixote tried to ride forward to help, but with two hundred angry men in his way all he could do was canter off, expecting at every moment to feel a crossbow bolt in his back.

The villagers slung the unconscious Sancho over his donkey's back and shooed it away, and by good luck it trotted off at once to join its great friend Rocinante.

The villagers waited until nightfall, and then, as no one turned up to fight them, they took themselves home quite cheerfully.

And that was the end of that.

The next day Don Quixote saw a fine lady out hunting, and ordered Sancho to offer her Don Quixote's services.

'Don Quixote?' said the lady. '*The* Don Quixote? How thrilling! You must come to stay at my husband the duke's castle.'

Well, when Don Quixote heard that the lady was a duchess he went to kneel at her feet. He would have made a more dignified job of it if he hadn't managed to fall off Rocinante on the way, but the duke himself came forward to help Don Quixote up again. The duke and duchess had both read Cervantes's brilliant *Don Quixote* book, and they thought it'd be great fun to treat Don Quixote just like a knight errant from the old stories.

'Beautiful lady—' began Don Quixote.

'Ah, but we must be careful if we're speaking of beauty,' said the duke. 'We mustn't forget the lovely Dulcinea, must we?'

'Well, whoever made Dulcinea didn't make such a botched job of the duchess, either, did he,' said Sancho.

Don Quixote was hugely embarrassed.

'No knight errant ever had such a foolish squire,' he said, apologetically.

'No, but he's funny,' said the duchess. 'Sancho, you must ride beside me.'

The duke sent messengers ahead, and Don Quixote was welcomed to the castle with shouts of acclamation.

'Welcome, greatest of all knights!'

Don Quixote and Sancho were ushered straight into the duke's magnificent rooms, but Sancho was so worried about leaving his donkey that he stopped to ask an old lady to see that the beast was fed and comfortable.

Unfortunately the old lady was the very important Doña Rodríguez, one of the duchess's chaperones. Doña Rodríguez was hugely offended, and called down all sorts of insults on Sancho. The duke and duchess found this tremendously funny.

'Keep *quiet*, can't you, Sancho?' said Don Quixote later, when he'd been dressed in the finest velvet by a bevy of servants. 'They'll think we're imposters! Don't you realize this is your opportunity for fame and fortune?'

Don Quixote's words had little effect on Sancho, however, for that night at dinner Sancho chatted away non-stop. The duke and duchess were very much amused, but Don Quixote was so embarrassed that in the end, to keep Sancho quiet, Don Quixote began recounting the many adventures they'd had together.

The duke was so impressed that he at once offered Sancho the governorship of one of his own spare isles. Sancho was thrilled to bits.

When his master had gone to bed, Sancho told the duchess Don Quixote's ridiculous story of Montesinos's cave.

'But if Don Quixote is a fool, then you must be even more foolish to follow him,' she said. 'Perhaps you won't make a very good governor, Sancho.'

'Oh, but I can't help but follow Don Quixote,' said Sancho, earnestly. 'He's confused, I know, but I'm fond of him. Look, if you think I won't make a good governor, then that's all right. I mean, I've managed without being a governor so far. And after all, farm labourers often make happier endings than kings.'

But the duchess told Sancho the duke always kept his promises, whatever happened.

'Ah well,' said Sancho. 'I'm kind by nature and pity the poor, so perhaps I'll be all right.'

A few days later, Don Quixote and Sancho were sitting in the garden with the duke and duchess and their courtiers when they heard mournful music, and a huge man with a white beard strode up and knelt before them.

'Great ones! My mistress, the Countess Trifaldi, asks to tell her tragic story to Don Quixote, the brave helper of ladies, widows and chaperones.'

Sancho snorted. He was still smarting from Doña Rodríguez's insults after the donkey incident.

'I don't know about chaperones,' he said. 'It's hardly worth going two steps to help a *chaperone*.'

'A chaperone's better than a stupid gossiping squire!'

snapped Doña Rodríguez – but then more music sounded and a veiled lady came forward.

'Hello, great ones,' she said, in a surprisingly deep voice. 'I'm sorry to bother you, but I'm so sad that I really don't know which way up I am, and that's a fact. It's all because of this dratted enchanter. You see, I was chaperone to the lovely Princess Antonomasia—'

'Not *another* chaperone!' muttered Sancho.

'—but, flattered by Clavijo the knight, I allowed him to visit the princess, and the upshot was that they ended up getting married. Well, this made the princess's mother Queen Maguncia so cross that we buried her three days later.'

'Did she die, then?' asked Sancho.

'Well, we were hardly going to bury her alive, were we? Anyway, as soon as she was buried, lo and behold, the giant Malumbrino – you know, the enchanter – appeared on a wooden horse on top of the grave, and straight away he turned the princess into a brass monkey, and Clavijo into a metal crocodile, and there they'll stay, he says, until the famous Don Quixote comes and fights him. And to make matters even worse the moment he'd finished speaking all the chaperones in the castle felt their faces prickling, and, before we knew it, this had happened!'

The lady threw back her veil to reveal a face bearing a great bushy beard, and promptly fainted.

'Great heavens!' declared Don Quixote. 'We must set off at once!'

But the bearded lady, hurriedly waking up, told him that that the giant Malumbrino was sending a flying wooden horse, just like in the old story, to make Don Quixote's journey easier.

'You shall sit on the saddle,' said the bearded lady, 'and your squire shall sit behind you.'

'*What*?' said Sancho. 'Get jolted black and blue for hundreds of miles just for a load of chaperones? Not likely!'

'We're worth more than squires!' snapped Doña Rodríguez – but then four hairy men ran up carrying a huge wooden horse. They dumped it in front of Don Quixote and rushed off again.

'You're not getting me on that thing,' said Sancho. 'I don't like heights—'

'That's all right,' said the bearded lady. 'You have to be blindfolded.'

'—and if I fall off it's going to take me years to walk home. And I've got an isle to govern!'

'Your isle won't go away, Sancho, however long you're gone,' said the duke.

So Don Quixote and Sancho were blindfolded and helped up onto the horse, and then Don Quixote turned the magic peg in the horse's neck (just like in the old stories) to make it fly.

At once, everyone started shouting, 'Wow, look at them go! Just like a bullet! Faster than an arrow!'

'Master,' said Sancho. 'If we're really going so fast, how come we can still hear the people shouting?'

'Enchantment, my dear Sancho. All enchantment!'

Don Quixote and Sancho clung on, with a wind like several pairs of bellows blowing in their faces, until (on the duke's orders, of course) someone crept up and lit the fuse of the fireworks that were packed inside the horse's belly.

The whole horse exploded instantly, and Don Quixote and Sancho went up with it.

When Don Quixote and Sancho finally opened their eyes, they found to their amazement that they'd been blown right back to the duke's garden, and that everyone around them was lying flat on the ground as if stunned.

Nearby, attached to a huge lance stuck in the ground, was a sign:

Don Quixote's bravery wins the day, it said. *The chaperones' beards have fallen off, and the princess and her husband are human again.*

Everyone was hugely impressed, especially when Sancho told them how small the earth had looked from the horse's back, and how much fun he'd had playing with the stars.

That night, Don Quixote said to Sancho, 'I'll believe all that about the stars if you'll believe me about the cave of Montesinos. All right?'

The next day Sancho was fitted out with his governor costume.

'I just hope you've learned something while you've been observing my knight-errantry,' said Don Quixote, gloomily, as Sancho prepared to set off, 'because, basically, Sancho, you're a dunderhead. Just don't forget to be kind, just, humble and generous. Tuck your shirt in. Cut your fingernails. Get up early. Keep secrets. Don't eat garlic. Don't burp … I only wish you could write.'

'That's all right, I'll pretend I've hurt my hand, then no one will realize.'

'I just hope you don't end up destroying the whole isle.'

'You don't really think I will, do you?' asked Sancho, suddenly worried. 'Because if you do, then I'd better stay here, after all. I'd much rather be poor than cause anyone harm.'

'My dear Sancho, perhaps you're worthy to be a governor, after all,' said Don Quixote. 'And perhaps you'll even succeed at it. Goodness usually does.'

Chapter Five

That afternoon Sancho set off for his isle. Amongst his retinue of servants was the man who'd pretended to be the Countess Trifaldi's bearded chaperone.

Sancho noticed the resemblance and resolved to keep an eye on him.

Sancho didn't actually know what an isle was, so it didn't strike him as odd that there was no water surrounding the town where he was taken. He was received with cheers and banners saying, *Long live Governor Don Sancho Panza!*

'Oh, I'm not a don,' said Sancho. 'Plain Sancho, that's me. Who are these two old men?'

'They've come for your judgement,' said the-man-who-looked-like-the-bearded-chaperone. 'The way you decide between them will show the people how wise you are.'

'Well, I'll do my best,' said Sancho. 'What's the matter?'

'Lord Governor,' said the first old man. 'I lent this man some money, but now he's saying he's already given it back.'

'I have, too!' said the other old man. 'And I'll swear to it!'

He gave his stick to the first old man to hold, grasped the governor's staff, and swore on his very life that the money had already been repaid.

The first old man was quite crestfallen. 'Well, I can't remember anything about it,' he said. 'But there, if he's sworn on his life, well, that's that.'

Then the second old man took back his stick and hobbled away as fast as he could.

Sancho sat pondering for a while, and then suddenly ordered the man with the stick to be brought back.

'Split open his stick!' he said. And there, inside the stick, was the borrowed money.

Well, after that the people revered Sancho as the wisest of men – which he would have been if he'd worked out the scam by himself. Actually, though, the priest at home had told him a similar story a little while before.

That evening Sancho was shown to his palace, where waiting for him was a table piled with food. He even had his very own doctor to care for him.

Sancho reached hungrily for some fruit, but the doctor tapped the fruit bowl and a servant whisked it away before Sancho could take anything.

The same thing happened with the veal and the partridges.

At that point Sancho demanded to know what on earth was going on.

'Lord Governor,' said the doctor. 'I cannot let you eat anything that might hurt you.'

'Well, how about the rabbit?'

'Meat from a furred animal? Definitely not. In fact all I can allow is a very small quantity of quince jelly.'

Sancho threw down his knife.

'Look, he said. 'If you're not careful, I'll get a cudgel and I'll knock every single doctor right out of this isle, starting with—'

Galloping hooves sounded outside, and someone shouted: 'A message for the governor!'

An enemy is planning to attack the isle, the message said. *There is also a plot to poison you. Do not sleep or eat at present.*

'We'd better throw all this food away, then,' said a servant. 'Oh, and Lord Governor! There's a man arrived on business.'

'Business?' said Sancho. 'At this time of day?'

'My Lord Governor—'

'Oh, all right. Send him in if you must.'

The man asked Sancho for six hundred gold pieces. Sancho threw him out.

Meanwhile, Don Quixote, who was missing Sancho very much, wrote to his old squire with much good advice about visiting prisons and helping the poor.

Being a governor isn't half what it's cracked up to be, Sancho replied. *I haven't made a penny, so far, and if it carries on like this much longer I'm going to starve to death.*

Sancho's wife Teresa was missing Sancho, too, so she was delighted when the duchess sent her a coral necklace and news of Sancho's new position.

'Sancho's a governor!' Teresa told everyone. 'I'll have to buy myself a carriage!'

The priest, the barber, and Sansón from the university didn't know what to think when they heard Teresa's news. The coral necklace was genuine, but how could this tale of duchesses and governorships possibly be true?

They asked the page who'd brought the duchess's message to dinner.

Back on the isle, Sancho was ravenous. The doctor had only allowed him some candied fruit for breakfast. Apparently, hunger sharpened the brain.

Outside, people were queueing up for judgement.

That morning Sancho heard the case of the bridge. The law said that every traveller had to say why he wanted to cross the town bridge. If he told the truth he was allowed to cross, but if he lied he was hanged. But what should be done with a man who said he wanted to cross the bridge so he could be hanged? If he were allowed to cross unharmed then he'd lied, and so he should be hanged; but if he was hanged then he'd told the truth, and so should be allowed to cross.

'Er ... what was that again?' said Sancho.

They explained it all again several times. At last Sancho

said: 'Well, he should be set free, then, shouldn't he, because doing good is better than doing harm.'

That judgement impressed his servants, so much that they gave Sancho a really good lunch – though they did this partly out of pity, too, because the plan was that Sancho was to be deposed that very night.

That afternoon, Sancho made seven excellent laws that are still in force on his isle to this very day.

Back at the castle, Doña Rodríguez the chaperone came to see Don Quixote in floods of tears because her daughter's fiancé had run away.

Well, the duke was absolutely thrilled to hear it. He began to arrange a fight between Don Quixote and the fiancé to settle the matter at once.

That evening, Sancho received a message from Teresa.

Dear Sancho,

Your news nearly sent me mad with happiness, and I believe every word even though the others don't and Sansón talks of coming to bring you both safely home. The only thing that could be better is if you were a tax collector, because they get their hands on real money.

Shall I buy a carriage? Everyone would know how important you are then.

Love, Teresa

Sancho was awakened in the night by the sound of clashing weapons.

'An attack!' shouted his servants, rushing in and tying two wooden shields to him, one on his front and one on his back, so that Sancho couldn't so much as bend his knees. He fell over almost immediately and lay helpless, his nose to the stone floor, while people ran about in the dark and stood on him.

By the time the 'attackers' had finally been beaten off, he was bruised all over.

Well, Sancho could put up with a lot, but enough was enough. He resigned as governor at once, loaded up his dear donkey, and set off back to find his master.

Soon after dark, he rode over the edge of a cliff.

He spent the long night lying groaning with pain, but when the sun came up he helped his donkey to its feet and gave it all the food he had. The only way out seemed to be into the mouth of a cave.

The cave was scary and dark and went on for miles. Then it suddenly came to a dead end.

'Help!' called Sancho. '*Help!*'

And at once above him, a well-loved voice said: 'Sancho's voice, coming up from the ground! Oh no, the dear fellow must be dead!'

But then the donkey brayed, and Sancho shouted some more, so Don Quixote went to get help.

And very happy they all were to see one another once more.

Chapter Six

A large crowd gathered to witness Don Quixote's fight with Doña Rodríguez's daughter's fiancé. (Actually, the real fiancé had left the country, but the duke had disguised one of his servants in armour and given him a lance, a horse, and instructions not to kill Don Quixote.)

Unfortunately, when the servant saw Doña Rodríguez's daughter, he fell so much in love with her that he threw away his lance.

'I give up!' he said. 'I can't face the great Don Quixote. I agree to marry the lady!'

The lady was rather surprised when he lifted his visor and proved to be a complete stranger, but she declared herself happy enough, and so it all turned out a great triumph for Don Quixote.

The next day Don Quixote and Sancho, carrying a present of a bag of gold from the duke, left the castle.

That night they stayed at an inn (Don Quixote seemed to have got over confusing inns and castles) and they were eating some stew when they heard a voice from the next room.

'This new *Don Quixote* book is terrible,' it said. 'Why, Don Quixote doesn't even love Dulcinea anymore!'

'Someone's written a new book about me where I

don't love Dulcinea?' shouted Don Quixote, rushing next door. 'Where is it?'

The man was thrilled to bits when he found out who Don Quixote was. He let Don Quixote have a look at his new *Don Quixote* book. It was truly awful: ungrammatical, unfunny and, most importantly, all the adventures in it were completely untrue.

'This book hasn't been written by the brilliant and truthful Cervantes,' said Sancho, indignantly. 'Some villain's using our fame to make money by printing a load of lies about us!'

'Despicable,' said Don Quixote.

'Hey, but I'll tell you something,' said Sancho. 'If it says we went to the joust at Saragossa then that's quite clever, because we haven't even done that yet.'

'And we won't do it, either,' said Don Quixote, grimly. 'We shall go to the joust at Barcelona, instead, just to prove that this terrible bogus book is nothing to do with the genuine Don Quixote!'

So when they set out the next morning, they headed for Barcelona, and they went along quite happily until they were ambushed by bandits. Don Quixote and Sancho would have lost everything if the bandit leader, a man called Roque, hadn't come along and been astonished at the sight of Don Quixote's ancient armour.

'Cheer up,' he said. 'You're only being robbed.'

'But I am Don Quixote!' exclaimed Don Quixote. 'I shouldn't have let myself be captured; I should have killed you all!'

Well, Roque was tickled pink to meet the famous Don Quixote and Sancho Panza. He sent a message about them to a friend of his in Barcelona, alerting him to Don Quixote's arrival, and then Roque led the knight errant and his faithful squire through the night along secret paths to the outskirts of the great city, where he embraced his new friends, gave Sancho a present of money, and rode away.

So Don Quixote and Sancho Panza first saw Barcelona as the sun rose. They saw the vast twinkling sea with its magnificent galleys fluttering with pennants, they heard cannons firing in salute, and they saw coming towards them a crowd of fine gentlemen on horseback.

As the gentlemen reached Don Quixote, their leader cried, 'Hail, Don Quixote, greatest of knights errant, whose tale we have read in Cervantes's fine book, though not in that terrible bogus sequel that some villain has just published! Welcome to Barcelona!'

Then Don Quixote and Sancho rode, escorted by all these fine gentlemen, to the house of their leader, who was called Don Antonio. And it was all very glorious indeed.

They had a sumptuous meal (Sancho thought he was

in heaven) and then Don Antonio took Don Quixote for a ride round the city. Don Antonio had secretly pinned a notice to Don Quixote's back which said, *This is Don Quixote de la Mancha.* Don Quixote was amazed to discover how famous he was.

That night Don Antonio held a ball, and so many ladies wanted to dance with Don Quixote that in the end he collapsed from sheer exhaustion and Sancho had to carry him to bed.

The next morning, as Don Quixote rode along the beach in full armour, he saw another knight riding towards him.

'Illustrious Don Quixote!' called the knight. 'I am the Knight of the White Moon. Admit that my lady is more beautiful than Dulcinea and we won't have to fight. But if we do fight, and I am the victor, then you must agree to go back quietly to your village and stay there for a year.'

The sight of two knights in armour preparing for battle soon drew an excited crowd. The White Moon knight had a much bigger and better horse than Rocinante, and so when he and Don Quixote met, he was travelling a lot faster than the Knight of the Lions. Even though the White Moon knight raised his lance at the last minute so as not to wound Don Quixote, the impact was awful. It swept Don Quixote and Rocinante away, over and over, in a terrible fall.

The White Moon knight dismounted and ran to put his lance at Don Quixote's throat.

'Surrender!' he said.

'No, no,' gasped Don Quixote. 'Dulcinea is the fairest lady in all Spain. You must kill me!'

'I will acknowledge her beauty if you will fulfil your promise to go home and stay there quietly for a year,' said the White Moon knight.

And to this Don Quixote, as an honest knight, was forced to agree. The White Moon knight cantered off into the city, leaving Don Quixote too injured to walk, Rocinante unable to get up, Sancho in despair, and everyone else agog to know who the White Moon knight might be.

Don Quixote was so badly hurt he was forced to go to bed for a week. He was very dejected, though Sancho did his best to cheer him up with plans about what they'd do after their year's retirement was over.

'I didn't like being a governor,' he said, 'but I wouldn't mind being a count.'

Don Antonio was determined to find out who the White Moon knight was, and of course (though Don Antonio promised to keep it secret), the White Moon knight was really our old friend Sansón from the university, who had finally managed to make Don Quixote go safely home.

Don Quixote left Barcelona wearing ordinary travelling clothes. His armour was packed on Sancho's donkey.

'Cheer up, Master,' said Sancho. 'Don't forget that a brave heart bears bad fortune just as well as good.'

'But everything I live for is finished if I can't be a knight errant, my friend.'

'Oh, the year will soon be over, and then we'll go off again.'

They rode on, sometimes sleeping under the stars and sometimes in inns (which Don Quixote always recognized; it seemed as if his defeat had caused his judgement to begin to return to him). In one inn, their room had a very bad painting on the wall of Princess Helen being kidnapped by Prince Paris of Troy.

'If only Helen had lived nowadays I could have saved her,' said Don Quixote, mournfully. 'I could have saved the whole city of Troy.'

'Don't worry,' said Sancho. 'Soon every inn in Spain will have a painting of us in it. And a better one than that stupid thing, too.'

'Yes, Sancho. That painter is about as good an artist as the villain who wrote that fake *Don Quixote* book.'

The next evening, Don Quixote and Sancho finally came within sight of their own village. There were men hunting with dogs in the fields, and as Don Quixote and

Sancho went along, a hare raced up to them.

Sancho caught it and gave it to Don Quixote.

'It is a sign,' said Don Quixote, very sad. 'The greyhounds can't catch the hare, and I shall never see Dulcinea's true face.'

'But how can me catching a hare mean that?' protested Sancho. 'Anyway, doesn't the priest always say all that sign stuff is nonsense?'

But Don Quixote didn't cheer up.

The priest, the barber and Sansón came out joyfully when they saw their old friends, and Don Quixote's niece and Teresa Panza escorted Don Quixote and Sancho firmly to their homes.

Teresa was surprised that Sancho wasn't riding a governor's fine horse, but she was delighted with the money Sancho had got from the duke and Roque the bandit.

Don Quixote told his friends the story of his defeat at the hands of the White Moon knight.

'Staying at home sounds extremely sensible to me,' said the housekeeper. 'You'll be able to take care of your property and your health.'

'My dears,' said Don Quixote, 'whatever I do, I shall take care of you. Now help me to my bed, for I don't feel very well.'

Don Quixote died quite suddenly. What caused his

fever, whether it was his defeat, or his disappointment at not seeing Dulcinea's true face, is not known. He lay in bed, very sad, and then suddenly he fell asleep and slept for six whole hours. When he awoke, he smiled at them, and told them he was sane again and that the spell cast by all those stories about knights and giants and enchanters had completely faded away.

'You must be happy,' he told them, 'for I'm no longer Don Quixote, but your old friend Alonso Quixano, whom some have called 'The Good'. I'm also the enemy of all knights errant.'

'Oh, don't be like that,' said Sansón. 'You're home, and you're safe, and you're soon going to be happy again.'

'I am soon going to be dead,' said Don Quixote (a.k.a. Alonso Quixano). 'And I must make my will.'

At that everyone cried a great deal because Don Quixote, whether mad or not, had always been so lovable and good.

'Forgive me for making you look mad yourself, Sancho,' said Don Quixote, when his friend visited him. 'All the money we got on our travels is yours.'

'Don't die!' sobbed Sancho. 'We'll travel again when this year's over, you'll see. Please don't die!'

Don Quixote left his house to his niece, on the condition that she didn't marry anyone who read books about knight-errantry, and he asked the forgiveness of the villainous writer of the fake *Don Quixote* book for prompting him to write something so truly terrible.

Don Quixote died three days later, and that was the end of the famous knight errant from the village whose name Cervantes couldn't quite recall, which piece of forgetfulness has left all the villages of La Mancha fighting for ever to claim that great man for themselves.

Farewell.